Alpine Cupcakes, Inc.

Audit Case Study

Carol Callaway Dee
University of Colorado Denver

Cindy Durtschi
DePaul University

Mary P. Mindak
DePaul University

Cambridge
BUSINESS PUBLISHERS

Cambridge Business Publishers

ALPINE CUPCAKES, INC. AUDIT CASE STUDY, First Edition, by Carol Callaway Dee, Cindy Durtschi, and Mary Mindak.

ISBN: 978-1-61853-073-8

Bookstores & Faculty: to order this book, call **800-619-6473** or email **customerservice@cambridgepub.com.**

TABLE OF CONTENTS

Preface

This casebook is a resource to use in the development of students' comprehension of critical auditing concepts. The casebook is suitable for both graduate and undergraduate students and can be used as a supplement to any auditing textbook. Students act as employees of Garcia and Foster, CPAs and conduct an internal inspection of the firm's audit of Alpine Cupcakes, Inc. Garcia and Foster is a fictitious regional firm with 20 offices located in large cities throughout the western United States. As part of its quality control procedures, the firm chooses five offices each year and conducts an internal inspection of a completed audit engagement.

The case assignments require students to *review* completed audit workpapers rather than *create* workpapers from scratch. This allows students to find errors in completed audit procedures and related documentation. For example, students identify weaknesses in the client's internal controls that the auditors failed to find, evaluate the auditors' tests of internal controls and substantive testing procedures, and assess the quality and completeness of the auditors' workpaper documentation.

This casebook provides students an opportunity to see realistic audit workpapers, visualize how audit workpapers are linked to the audit program, and learn how source documents are integrated into audit tasks. Students practice critical thinking skills as they consider the purpose of audit procedures and the issues that arise when trying to implement those procedures in a realistic setting.

Although Alpine Cupcakes, Inc. is a fictitious company, we generated the accounting records in the casebook by creating over 2 years of realistic transactions for a company that manufactures and sells cupcakes. Thus, the underlying client source documents are representative of actual transactions, providing students the opportunity to observe the association between audit workpapers and realistic client documents. This realism is valuable to students, especially given the revised approach to the auditing portion of the CPA exam, in which the AICPA adds document review simulations.

The casebook contains three modules (risk assessment, cash, and accounts receivable). Each module can be used independently; in addition, portions of modules or specific questions within modules can be chosen by the instructor. The risk assessment module focuses on preliminary analytical procedures, materiality estimation, and applying the audit risk model. The cash module contains a comprehensive audit of cash, including evaluation of internal controls over cash receipts and disbursements, test of control procedures, and substantive testing. The accounts receivable module incorporates consideration of the sales revenue and accounts receivable processes, including processes related to the company's estimation of uncollectible accounts. Students will evaluate the auditor's test of control and substantive testing over the sales and accounts receivable processes and transactions.

Acknowledgments

This casebook has benefited greatly from the comments of focus group attendees, reviewers, and colleagues. We thank our colleagues at DePaul University and University of Colorado Denver. Special thanks go to Marsha Keune (University of Dayton) and the students at DePaul University and University of Colorado Denver who completed many early versions of the cases and provided valuable feedback. We are extremely grateful for their care, attention, and support.

Thank you to the reviewers in our focus group at the 2015 American Accounting Association Annual Meeting, including Barbara Arel (The University of Vermont), Lisa Baudot (University of Central Florida), Tina Carpenter (University of Georgia), Meghann Cefaratti (Northern Illinois University), Shifei Chung (Rowan University), Donna Free (Oakland University), Barbara Grein (Drexel University), Jennifer Joe (University of Delaware), Jacquelyn Sue Moffitt (Louisiana State University), Pamela Roush (University of Central Florida), and Timothy Seidel (Brigham Young University).

Thank you to the additional reviewers, including Cynthia Bolt-Lee (The Citadel), Holly Caldwell (Bridgewater College), Lawrence Chui (University of St. Thomas), Donald R. Deis (Texas A&M University – Corpus Christi), Thomas Dowdell, Jr. (North Dakota State University), Robert Eger (Naval Postgraduate School), Diana Franz (University of Toledo), Cindy Guthrie (Bucknell University), Julia Higgs (Florida Atlantic University), Jason MacGregor (Baylor University), Edward W. Machir (Georgetown University), Diane Matson (University of St. Thomas), Roger Mayer (SUNY Old Westbury), Linda McCann (Metropolitan State University), Kathy R. O'Donnell (University at Buffalo), Susan Parker (Santa Clara University), Vernon Richardson (University of Arkansas), Laura Simeoni (York University), Richard Walstra (Dominican University), Donna Whitten (Purdue University North Central), and Angela Woodland (Montana State University).

Thank you to our research assistants at DePaul University for their work on the casebook, including Fangfang Li, Michael Lauridsen, Sahar Mohammad, and Matthew Kalina.

In addition, we are grateful to George Werthman, Marnee Fieldman, Jill Sternard, Susan McIntyre, and the entire team at Cambridge Business Publishers for their encouragement, enthusiasm, guidance, and patience.

Carol Callaway Dee   *Cindy Durtschi*   *Mary P. Mindak*

About the Authors

Carol Callaway Dee is an associate professor of accounting in the Business School at the University of Colorado Denver. Prior to coming to CU Denver, she was on the faculty of Florida State University. She earned her PhD in accounting from Louisiana State University and a BS in accounting from the University of Florida. Dr. Dee was an academic fellow for the Public Company Accounting Oversight Board's Office of Research and Analysis and its Center for Economic Analysis, conducting research on the economic effects of proposed auditing standards. She has published in a number of journals, including *The Accounting Review, Contemporary Accounting Research, Current Issues in Auditing, Issues in Accounting Education,* and *Journal of Accounting and Public Policy,* and she serves as an associate editor for the *Journal of Forensic Accounting Research.* Her accounting cases, *Return of the Tallahassee BeanCounters: A Case in Forensic Accounting* (with Cindy Durtschi) and *Grand Teton Candy Company: Connecting the Dots in a Fraud Case* (with Cindy Durtschi and Mary Mindak) are used by faculty around the world. She is a recipient of the CU Denver Business School's "Outstanding Tenure-Track Teacher of the Year" Award.

Cindy Durtschi is an associate professor of accounting at the Driehaus College of Business, DePaul University, where she directs the Masters in Accountancy program. She received her PhD from the University of Arizona. Prior to arriving at DePaul University, she held positions at Florida State University and Utah State University. Dr. Durtschi teaches forensic accounting in the MACC program at DePaul as well as financial accounting in both the MSA and MBA programs. She has won the Gus Economos Distinguished Teaching Award for the Kellstadt Graduate School of Business at DePaul University, the Teacher of the Year for the Huntsman College of Business at Utah State University, and Outstanding Teacher Award for the Department of Finance at the University of Arizona. Dr. Durtschi's research is published in *Journal of Accounting Research, Journal of Accounting, Auditing and Finance, Journal of Forensic Accounting, Issues in Accounting Education, and the Journal of Forensic Accounting,* as well as other journals. She received the 2006 American Accounting Association Innovation in Audit Education Award for her first published case in forensic accounting, *The Tallahassee BeanCounters: A Problem-Based Learning Case in Forensic Auditing*. She continues to publish forensic accounting cases (now with Carol Callaway Dee, Mary Mindak, and/or Robert Rufus) that are used in classrooms around the world. Dr. Durtschi is currently on the editorial boards of *Issues in Accounting Education, Journal of Forensic and Investigative Accounting,* and *Journal of Accounting and Free Enterprise*. She is past president of the Forensic Accounting Section of the American Accounting Association.

Mary P. Mindak is an assistant professor of accounting in the Driehaus College of Business at DePaul University. She graduated from Miami University with a BS in Accountancy and a Masters of Accountancy and received her PhD from the University of Cincinnati. Professor Mindak worked at Ernst & Young as an auditor in the Financial Services and Healthcare industries. She also worked in corporate accounting at Western & Southern Life Insurance Company. Dr. Mindak's research focuses on areas affecting audit risk, including aggressive reporting, earnings management, fraud, bankruptcy, and corporate responsibility. Her work has been published in *Issues in Accounting Education, Research in Accounting Regulation, Managerial Auditing Journal, Journal of Accounting Ethics and Public Policy,* and *The CPA Journal*. She currently teaches Auditing and Financial Reporting at DePaul University. She is the faculty advisor for DECA (a student organization with multiple case competitions each year) and the PwC Corporate Challenge Case Competition.

Garcia and Foster, CPAs, and Their 20X2 Audit of Alpine Cupcakes, Inc.

Introduction: Garcia and Foster, CPAs, is a regional firm with 20 offices located in large cities throughout the western United States. As part of its quality control procedures, the firm chooses 5 offices each year and conducts an internal inspection of a completed audit engagement. The internal inspection process helps Garcia and Foster ensure the consistent application of audit firm practices and auditing standards, and efficiently modifies firm practices to improve audit quality and reduce the likelihood of an audit failure.

Garcia and Foster Audit Process

1. Step 1 is audit planning, in which the audit team develops the auditing strategies and procedures for the client after the auditor has considered client acceptance or continuance. The audit team assesses the previous year's audit program and revises it as needed for the current year's engagement. In addition, the firm sends an audit engagement letter to the client, establishing the services that the firm will provide to the client. Once signed by the client, this letter acts as a contract between the audit firm and the client.
2. Step 2 requires the audit team to obtain and document its understanding of the client's environment, including internal controls. This understanding allows the auditors to identify significant risks in the audit engagement. During this phase, the auditors determine materiality and perform preliminary analytical procedures.
3. In Step 3, the audit team uses information obtained in Step 2 to determine the risks of material misstatement on the audit engagement—both overall financial statement risks, and risks at the individual account level. These risk assessment procedures guide the auditor in altering, if necessary, the audit program in response to the assessed risks.
4. Next, in Step 4, the audit team tests internal controls and performs substantive procedures to obtain the audit evidence needed to form an opinion on the financial statements.
5. In Step 5, the auditor performs additional procedures typically done at the end of the audit, such as searching for unrecorded liabilities, reviewing attorneys' letters, and obtaining a management representation letter from the client. The auditor reviews the overall audit evidence and conclusions to determine the audit opinion.
6. Finally, the auditor issues the audit opinion. After the engagement is complete, planning can begin for next year's audit (Step 1).

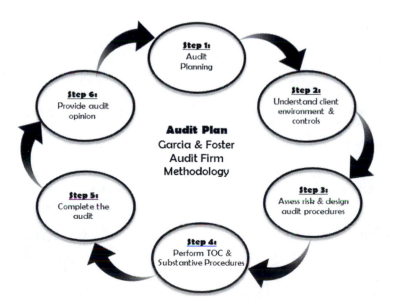

Objective: You are a senior audit manager with Garcia and Foster, based in the Salt Lake City, Utah office. You are in charge of conducting an internal inspection of the Denver, Colorado office. As part of your work, you are examining and evaluating the audit evidence and documentation for the 20X2 audit of Alpine Cupcakes, Inc.

Risk Assessment Module

Introduction:

The risk assessment module focuses on several important assessment procedures. One of the main objectives of this module is to have you review and gain a better understanding of preliminary analytical procedures. Through reviewing these documents, you will see real world audit workpapers and have the opportunity to assess the auditors' performance of the required procedures. In addition, you will be able to consider Alpine Cupcake's overall financial statement risk and the account level risks as you review the workpapers. The audit workpapers also include audit documentation on the auditors' materiality calculations and overall risk assessment of inherent risk, control risk, and detection risk. Through this module, you will gain a better understanding of the auditors' considerations of client risk and how this assessment affects the audit.

Learning Objectives:

The goal of this module is to enable you to understand the auditors' audit planning and risk assessment procedures. After performance of the module, you will be able to:
1. Assess the auditors' documentation of their understanding of the client's environment, including its internal controls.
2. Review and evaluate the auditors' materiality threshold calculations.
3. Understand and apply the audit risk model.
4. Review and evaluate the auditors' preliminary analytical procedures.
5. Evaluate the auditors' documentation of their risk assessment procedures.
6. Conduct research on auditing standards for audits of nonpublic companies.

Assignment:

Before beginning the assignment, take a moment to look through the papers in this module. Note in the lower left-hand corner that some documents are audit work papers created by Garcia and Foster CPAs as they conducted the audit. Note that other papers are client documents that Garcia and Foster collected and kept in support of their audit. Finally, note the numbering system in the lower right-hand corner of each page and how each paper within the audit is numbered and linked back to the audit program.

In this part of your assignment, you will examine the firm's audit documentation in relation to the auditors' performance on several risk assessment procedures. Please complete the following tasks:

Q1. Research, cite, and summarize (in one or two sentences per standard identified) the auditing standards as they relate to the auditors' responsibilities in the following areas:
   a. Obtaining and documenting an understanding of the client's environment, including internal controls.
   b. Materiality assessment in planning and performing the audit.
   c. The audit risk model.
   d. Preliminary analytical procedures.

Q2. Evaluate Garcia and Foster's documentation of their understanding of the client's environment (workpaper B.2.1.) Describe any problems you find and provide suggestions for improvement. This question relates to Step 2 of the Garcia and Foster Audit Plan.

Q3. Review Garcia and Foster's calculations of materiality thresholds for the 20X2 Audit (workpaper B.2.1.) Determine if the auditors correctly applied the materiality concept in their risk assessment procedures. Describe any problems you find and provide suggestions for improvement. This question relates to Step 2 of the Garcia and Foster Audit Plan.

Q4. Evaluate other aspects of the Audit Risk Assessment memo (workpaper B.2.1.) In particular, review the auditors' application of the audit risk model and brainstorming processes. Describe any problems you find and provide suggestions for improvement. Identify and document any additional problems you discover with the memo. This question relates to Step 3 of the Garcia and Foster Audit Plan.

Case Assignment: Pg. pg. 2 of 5

Q5. Evaluate the preliminary analytical procedures completed by Garcia and Foster, CPAs (workpapers B.3.1 to B.3.3.) This question relates to Step 2 of the Garcia and Foster Audit Plan.
   a. Determine if the analyses of account fluctuations were appropriately performed and completed (workpapers B.3.1 and B.3.2). Review the explanations of account fluctuations provided by the auditors. Describe any problems you identify.
   b. Determine if the ratio analysis (workpaper B.3.3) was appropriately performed and completed. Review the explanations of ratio fluctuations provided by the auditors. Describe any problems you identify.

⌐→ do they make sense

Q6. Prepare a memo to document your understanding of Alpine Cupcakes, Inc.'s environment and provide your assessment of Garcia and Foster's audit risk. Describe the specific risks for Alpine Cupcakes, Inc., explain why you believe these factors relate to the Alpine Cupcakes audit, and identify which specific accounts are likely to be affected by these risks. Describe how the audit teams should address the risks identified. For example, the background information mentions that sugar prices may rise. What risks would this present to Alpine Cupcakes? Which accounts would be affected by this risk? How should the audit team address these risks in the audit plan?

Client background

pg 33 & 34

Cash Module

Introduction:
The cash module is a comprehensive coverage of the cash account, along with the related processes. Within this module, you will gain a better understanding of important procedures performed by auditors in relation to the cash account and processes. This module includes consideration of both the cash receipt and cash disbursement processes. You will have the opportunity to review the narrative of cash processes to identify weaknesses in Alpine's internal controls. Your assessment of the auditors' testing of controls procedures will allow you to understand the testing of controls procedures and auditor documentation in relation to the cash processes. You will be able to investigate and examine the auditors' procedures with important substantive tests, including bank reconciliations and cash confirmations. Through this module, you will gain a better understanding of typical audit procedures along with common issues that could occur in the auditing of the cash account.

Learning Objectives:

The goal of this module is to enhance your understanding of cash audit procedures, including cash receipt and cash disbursement processes. After performance of the module, you will be able to:
   1. Identify internal control weaknesses in the client's cash processes.
   2. Review and evaluate the auditors' testing of internal controls over the cash processes.
   3. Assess the substantive testing over the cash confirmation procedures.
   4. Evaluate the substantive testing over the bank reconciliation procedures.
   5. Identify any red flags for the potential of material misstatement in the cash accounts.

Assignment:
Before beginning the assignment, take a moment to look through the papers in this module. Note in the lower left-hand corner that some documents are audit work papers created by Garcia and Foster CPAs as they conducted the audit. Note that other papers are client documents that Garcia and Foster collected and kept in support of their audit. Finally, note the numbering system in the lower right-hand corner and how each paper within the audit is numbered and linked back to the audit program.

In this part of your assignment, you will examine the firm's audit documentation in relation to the audit of Alpine's cash balance and related cash processes. Please complete the following tasks:
1. Research, cite, and summarize (in one or two sentences per standard identified) the auditing standards that address Garcia and Foster, CPA's, responsibility in relation to evaluating Alpine's internal controls. Identify the most relevant paragraph(s) in each standard.
2. Review the cash narrative memo (C.1.1) and cash flowcharts (C.1.2). Identify and document any internal control weaknesses over cash receipts, cash disbursements, bank reconciliation, and/or petty cash. Explain why each item identified is a weakness. This question relates to Step 2 of the Garcia and Foster Audit Plan.

Pg. 47

3. Based on your review of the cash testing of controls procedures (workpapers C.2.1 to C.2.11), you believe that there were some issues with the audit work performed. Review in detail the auditing procedures from the audit program and the related documentation.
Identify any of the following issues:
   a. Did they perform all of the steps associated with the audit program?
   b. Did they perform the steps accurately? If not, describe the problem and follow up on it to the extent possible with the information given.
   c. Do you see any other issues or problems with the auditors' work or client documentation?
   This question relates to Step 4 of the Garcia and Foster Audit Plan.
4. You have concerns about the adequacy of the substantive audit work done by the engagement team. Review in detail the cash confirmation and bank reconciliation substantive audit program steps (C.3 and C.4) and the associated audit workpapers (C.3.1 to C.4.8).
Identify any of the following issues:
   a. Did they perform all of the steps associated with the audit program?
   b. Did they perform the steps accurately? If not, describe the problem and follow up on it to the extent possible with the information given.
   c. Do you see any other issues or problems with the auditors' work or client documentation?
   This question relates to Step 4 of the Garcia and Foster Audit Plan
5. Write a professional memo to the engagement partner (Anna Garcia) summarizing your findings for questions 2, 3, and 4. The memo should be 1 page or less single-spaced.
   a. Identify the areas of the audit that need improvements.
   b. Provide feedback on ways to improve their audit of the cash account.
   c. Use constructive criticism. Remember that the purpose of Garcia and Foster's internal inspection program is not punitive. Rather, the goal of the program is to improve the quality of the firm's audit work.

Accounts Receivable and Sales Module

Introduction:
The accounts receivable module incorporates consideration of the sales revenue and accounts receivable processes, including processes related to the Alpine's allowance for uncollectable accounts. This module will help you gain a better understanding of the audit procedures, audit workpapers, and client documents that relate to these processes. In this module, you will consider and evaluate the internal control weaknesses by reviewing the accounts receivable and sales narrative. You will have the opportunity to review and assess the auditors' tests of controls procedures over the sales and accounts receivable processes. This module further asks you to investigate and examine important procedures including substantive testing of the accounts receivable aging list, sales cutoff, and the allowance for uncollectible accounts. Through this module, you will gain a better understanding of typical audit procedures, along with common issues that could occur in the auditing of the sales and accounts receivable account balances and processes.

Learning Objectives:
This module enhances your understanding of the audit procedures for the client's accounts receivable and sales transactions. After performance of the module, you will be able to:
1. Conduct research on auditing standards in relation to the use of external confirmations to evaluate the accounts receivable balance and the allowance for uncollectible accounts.
2. Evaluate the auditors' procedures to understand internal controls over the sales, accounts receivable and allowance for uncollectible accounts processes.
3. Review and evaluate the auditors' testing of internal controls over the sales, accounts receivable, and allowance for uncollectible accounts processes.
4. Evaluate the substantive testing of sales and AR including cutoff testing of sales transactions.
5. Review the substantive audit procedures performed to test to the client's allowance for uncollectible accounts balance.

Assignment:

Before beginning the assignment, take a moment to look through the papers in this module. Note in the lower left-hand corner that some documents are audit work papers created by Garcia and Foster CPAs as they conducted the audit. Note that other papers are client documents that Garcia and Foster collected and kept in support of their audit. Finally, note the numbering system in the lower right-hand corner and how each paper within the audit is numbered and linked back to the audit program.

In this part of your assignment, you will examine the firm's audit documentation in relation to the audit of Alpine's accounts receivable and sales processes and accounts. Please complete the following tasks:

Q1. Research, cite, and summarize (in one or two sentences per standard identified) the auditing standards that address Garcia and Foster, CPA's, responsibility in relation to sending accounts receivable confirmations. Identify the most relevant paragraph(s) in each standard.

Q2. Review the accounts receivable narrative (AR.1.1) and review the accounts receivable flowchart (AR.1.2) to identify all of the internal control weaknesses for the accounts receivable and sales processes. Provide one or two sentences on why each item identified is a weakness. This question relates to Step 2 of the Garcia and Foster Audit Plan.

Q3. Based on your review of the accounts receivable test of controls procedures (workpapers AR.2.1 to AR.2.4), you believe that there were some issues with the audit work performed. Review in detail the auditing procedures from the audit program and the related documentation. Pay particular attention to their implementation of the attribute sampling procedures—their sample selection process and evaluation of the results. Identify any of the following issues:

    a. Did they perform all of the steps associated with the audit program?

    b. Did they perform the steps accurately? If not, specifically state the nature of the problem and follow up on it to the extent possible with the information given.

    c. Do you see any other issues or problems with the auditors' work or client documentation?

This question relates to Step 4 of the Garcia and Foster Audit Plan.

Q4. Review the accounts receivable lead sheet memo and related workpapers (AR.3.1 to AR.3.4). Evaluate the auditors' tickmarks, comments, and explanations in the memo and on the lead sheet. Identify any of the following issues:

    a. Did they perform all of the steps associated with the AR.3 audit procedure?

    b. Did they perform the steps accurately? If not, specifically state the nature of the problem and follow up on it to the extent possible with the information given.

    c. Do you see any other issues or problems with the auditors' work or client documentation?

This question relates to Step 4 of the Garcia and Foster Audit Plan.

Q5. You are also concerned about the adequacy of the substantive audit work done by Garcia and Foster. You decide to carefully review the substantive testing performed on the aged accounts receivable summary (AR.4.1 to AR.4.5), accounts receivable confirmation testing (AR.5.1 to AR.5.8), sales cutoff testing (AR.6.1 to AR.6.7), and the testing of the allowance for uncollectible accounts (AR.7.1). Identify any of the following issues:

    a. Did they perform all of the steps associated with the audit program?

    b. Did they perform the steps accurately? If not, specifically state the nature of the problem and follow up on it to the extent possible with the information given.

    c. Do you see any other issues or problems with the auditors' work or client documentation?

This question relates to Step 4 of the Garcia and Foster Audit Plan.

Q6. After answering the above questions, write a professional memo to the audit engagement partner (Anna Garcia) summarizing your findings for questions 2, 3, 4, and 5. The memo should be 1 page or less single-spaced.

    a. Identify the areas of the audit that need improvement.

    b. Provide feedback on ways to improve their audit of the accounts receivable and sales accounts.

    c. Use constructive criticism. Remember that the purpose of Garcia and Foster's internal inspection program is not punitive. Rather, the goal of the program is to improve the quality of the firm's audit work.

Garcia and Foster, CPAs, LLC

1790 Lawrence St., Denver, CO 80202

Audit Workpapers

Client:	Alpine Cupcakes, Inc.
Balance Sheet Date:	December 31, 20X2
Engagement Partner:	Anna Garcia
Fieldwork ended:	February 25, 20X3
Audit Report date:	February 25, 20X3
Second Partner Review Completed:	Evan Foster 2/25/20X3
Document Completion Date:	February 25, 20X3

Alpine Cupcakes, Inc.
Workpapers Index
Audit Year December 31, 20X2

Index of workpapers included for review:

Module	Reference	Title
Accounting Records and Engagement Files		
	Audit Program	Audit Program—Audit Year December 31, 20X2
	ADMIN	Audit Engagement Team Staffing and Guidelines
	A.1.1	Engagement Letter
	A.1.2	Management Representation Letter
	A.1.3	Audit Opinion
	A.1.4	Balance Sheets as of 12/31/20X2 and 12/31/20X1
	A.1.5	Income Statements for the 12 Months Ended 12/31/20X2, 12/31/20X1, and 12/31/20X0
	A.1.6	Statements of Stockholders' Equity for the Years Ended 12/31/20X2 and 12/31/20X1
	A.1.7	Statements of Cash Flows for the Years Ended 12/31/20X2, 12/31/20X1, and 12/31/20X0
	A.1.8	Notes to Financial Statements—December 31, 20X2
	A.1.9	Trial Balance—December 31, 20X2
	Background	Client Background
	ORG CHART	Organizational Chart
Risk Assessment Module		
	B.1.1	Balance Sheets as of 3/31/20X2 and 12/31/20X1
	B.1.2	Income Statements for the 3 Months Ended 3/31/20X2 and 3/31/20X1
	B.2.1	Audit Risk Assessment Memo
	B.3.1	Preliminary Analytical Procedures—Balance Sheets
	B.3.2	Preliminary Analytical Procedures—Quarterly Income Statements
	B.3.3	Preliminary Analytical Procedures—Ratio Analysis
Cash Module—Understanding Internal Controls (Cash Q2)		
	C.1.1	Cash Narrative
	C.1.2	Cash Flowcharts
Cash Module—Test of Internal Controls (Cash Q3)		
	C.2.1	Cash Receipts, Disbursements, and Reconciliation TOC Memo
	C.2.2	Mailroom Control Listing—October 20X2
	C.2.3	Mailroom Control Listing—December 20X2
	C.2.4	Mountain Dairy Company Voucher Packet
	C.2.5	Denver Office Supplies Voucher Packet
	C.2.6	Cynthia Jamison Voucher Packet
	C.2.7	Rocky Mountain Kitchen Goods Voucher Packet
	C.2.8	Milsap Foods Voucher Packet
	C.2.9	Payroll Transfer Voucher Packet
	C.2.10	Operating Cash Account Reconciliation—October 31, 20X2
	C.2.11	Operating Cash Account Reconciliation—November 30, 20X2
Cash Module—Substantive Testing (Cash Q4)		
	C.3.1	Cash Confirmation Memo
	C.3.2	Alpine Standard Bank Confirmation—Copy

Garcia and Foster Audit Workpaper

Module	Reference	Title
Cash Module—Substantive Testing Continued (Cash Q4)		
	C.3.3	Alpine Standard Bank Confirmation—December 20X2
	C.4.1	Bank Reconciliation Memo
	C.4.2	Operating Cash Account Reconciliation—December 31, 20X2
	C.4.3	Operating Outstanding Check and DIT Listing—December 31, 20X2
	C.4.4	Operating Cash Bank Statement—December 31, 20X2
	C.4.5	Operating Cash Bank Statement—January 31, 20X3
	C.4.6	Operating Outstanding Check and DIT Listing—November 30, 20X2
	C.4.7	Cash Receipts Journal—Corporate Account—December 20X2
	C.4.8	Check Log—Corporate Cash Account—December 20X2
	C.5.1	Presentation and Disclosure Memo
Accounts Receivable & Sales Module—Understanding Internal Controls (AR Q2)		
	AR.1.1	Sales and AR Narrative and Walkthrough
	AR.1.2	Corporate Sales and AR Flowchart
Accounts Receivable & Sales Module—Test of Internal Controls (AR Q3)		
	AR.2.1	AR TOC Memo
	AR.2.2	20X2 Sales Journal Excerpt
	AR.2.3	Boulder Tea House TOC Documents
	AR.2.4	High Country Coffee TOC Documents
Accounts Receivable & Sales Module—Substantive Testing (AR Q4)		
	AR.3.1	AR Lead Sheet Memo
	AR.3.2	AR Lead Sheet
	AR.3.3	20X2 Cupcake Corporate Sales Analysis
	AR.3.4	20X2 Monthly Sales Analysis
Accounts Receivable & Sales Module—Substantive Testing (AR Q5)		
	AR.4.1	20X2 AR Aging Auditor Memo
	AR.4.2	20X2 AR Aging Schedule
	AR.4.3	AR Aging Substantive Testing—Denver Bakery
	AR.4.4	AR Aging Substantive Testing—Luigi's Bistro
	AR.4.5	AR Aging Substantive Testing—Buckhead Restaurants
	AR.5.1	AR Confirmation Memo and Log
	AR.5.2	AR Confirmation Letters—Mile High Steak House
	AR.5.3	AR Confirmation Letters—Bon Appetito Restaurants
	AR.5.4	AR Confirmation Letters—UC Boulder Food Service
	AR.5.5	AR Confirmation Letters—Buckhead Restaurants
	AR.5.6	AR Confirmation Letters—The Sandwich Place
	AR.5.7	Mailroom Control Listing—January 20X3
	AR.5.8	General Ledger Journal Entries
	AR.6.1	Sales Cutoff Testing Memo
	AR.6.2	Sales Cutoff Testing—Smokey's Before Year End
	AR.6.3	Sales Cutoff Testing—Smokey's After Year End

Alpine Cupcakes, Inc.
Workpapers Index
Audit Year December 31, 20X2

Module	Reference	Title
Accounts Receivable & Sales Module—Substantive Testing Continued (AR Q5)		
	AR.6.4	Sales Cutoff Testing—Country Barrel Before Year End
	AR.6.5	Sales Cutoff Testing—Country Barrel After Year End
	AR.6.6	Sales Journal—December 20X2
	AR.6.7	Sales Journal—January 20X3
	AR.7.1	Accounts Receivable and Allowance for Uncollectible Accounts Memo

No.	Audit Procedure	By	Date	WP Ref. #
A.1	**Include relevant financial statement information in workpapers.**			
	A. Include Alpine Cupcakes, Inc. Financial Statements for years ended 12/31/20X2 and 12/31/20X1.	TES	02/25/20X3	A.1.4-1.7
	B. Include the December 31, 20X2 Trial Balance.	TES	02/25/20X3	A.1.9
B.1	**Obtain additional financial data**			
	A. Obtain the following financial statement data for the most recent quarters: Balance sheets for most recent quarter and 12/31/20X1 and Income Statements for most recent quarter and corresponding prior year's quarterly data.	SDM	9/15/20x2	B.1.1-1.2
B.2	**Perform risk assessment procedures.**			
	A. Using Garcia & Foster methodology, set the Planning Materiality (PM), Tolerable Misstatement (TM), and Summary of Audit Difference (SAD) thresholds for the 20X2 Alpine Audit.	SDM	9/15/20x2	B.2.1
	B. Obtain an understanding of the client and its environment, including internal controls.	SDM	9/15/20x2	B.2.1
	C. Determine the levels of inherent risk, control risk, and detection risk.	SDM	9/15/20x2	B.2.1
B.3	**Perform preliminary analytical procedures.**			
	A. Use Alpine's 2nd quarter 20X2 data (if available) to determine if there are any accounts with unusual fluctuations. The firm's strategy identifies unusual fluctuations as a change in the account from prior year where the dollar change is greater than TM and percentage change is greater than 10%.	SDM	10/01/20X2 *before year end*	B.3.1-3.2
	i. Discuss with management any accounts with unusual fluctuations to determine the reasons for these changes.			
	ii. Identify any potential risk (misstatements) that could occur to cause these changes.		*pg. 41-43*	

No.	Audit Procedure	By	Date	WP Ref. #
B.3	**Perform preliminary analytical procedures (continued).**			

	B. Perform a ratio analysis on Q1 20X2 data that identifies any unusual changes in the company's financial statement account balances. The firm's strategy identifies unusual ratios as a 10% change in the ratio from prior year. Our firm methodology also identifies any ratios that are outside of the min and max industry range as a potential red flag. _pg. 45_
	    i. Document the analysis and explain the significant fluctuations.
	    ii. Identify any potential risk (misstatements) that could occur in these related accounts to cause the change or difference from prior year and/or industry norms.
		SDM	10/01/20X2	B.3.3

C.1	**Understanding internal controls over the cash processes.**			
	A. Interview appropriate personnel to understand the cash receipts and disbursements process.	ARO	1/15/20X3	C.1.1
	B. Document the interview and responses in a cash receipts and disbursements narrative and flowchart.	ARO	1/15/20X3	C.1.1-1.2
C.2	**Test internal controls over cash receipts and cash disbursements.**			
	A. Test the mailroom control listing by obtaining the October and December monthly control listing logs from Diana Hayes. Determine if the following controls were performed:	ARO	2/4/20X3	C.2.1
	i. Lindsay McKenna reconciles the total on the monthly control listing to the Cash Receipts Subledger and General Ledger (GL).	ARO	2/4/20X3	C.2.2-2.3
	ii. Diana inputs the entries on a daily basis. Perform a surprise check to see if she has inputted all of the checks for the day.	ARO	2/4/20X3	C.2.2-2.3
	iii. Miguel Lopez reviews and signs off on the monthly control listing by the 2nd day of the following month.	ARO	2/4/20X3	C.2.2-2.3
	iv. Copies of the mailroom control listing are forwarded to the cashier and Accounts Receivable (AR) departments.			
	v. A reconciliation is performed between the mailroom control listing and the daily deposit slips.			

No.	Audit Procedure	By	Date	WP Ref. #
C.2	**Test internal controls over cash receipts and cash disbursements (continued).**			
	B. Obtain 6 cash disbursements made during the month of December to determine if the following controls are operating effectively:	ARO	2/4/20X3	C.2.1
	i. The company employees follow the proper authorization limits where Miguel Lopez signs any checks under $5,000 and Alexis Madison co-signs (along with Miguel) any checks over $5,000.	ARO	2/4/20X3	C.2.4-2.9
	ii. The company creates a voucher packet with the purchase order, vendor invoice, and the receiving report.	ARO	2/4/20X3	C.2.4-2.9
	iii. Miguel Lopez cancels supporting documents with a PAID stamp, the date of payment, and the signature of the person signing the check.	ARO	2/4/20X3	C.2.4-2.9
	C. Obtain the October and November cash operating account reconciliations. Determine if the following controls were properly applied:	ARO	2/4/20X3	C.2.10-2.11
	i. Lindsay McKenna prepares the account reconciliation on a monthly basis.	ARO	2/4/20X3	C.2.10-2.11
	ii. The bank reconciliation is performed within 5 days of month end.	ARO	2/4/20X3	C.2.10-2.11
	iii. The reconciliation is reviewed by Miguel Lopez within 10 days of month end.	ARO	2/4/20X3	C.2.10-2.11
	iv. Unreconcilable differences are investigated by Lindsay McKenna in a timely manner.	ARO	2/4/20X3	C.2.10-2.11
C.3	**Perform cash testing—bank confirmations.**			
	A. Identify the material cash balances held in bank accounts and provide a memo on the confirmation auditing procedures.	ARO	1/18/20X3	C.3.1
	B. Have the client complete cash standard bank confirmations for significant checking accounts. Validate the bank information.	ARO	1/18/20X3	C.3.2
	C. Create and document the cash confirmation process in a cash confirmation control listing.	ARO	1/18/20X3	C.3.1
	D. Send out confirmations directly to the bank(s). The client should not send the confirmation. Document your procedures and actions in the confirmation memo.	ARO	1/18/20X3	C.3.1
	E. Once the confirmations are received directly from the bank, document and set aside for use in testing the client's bank reconciliation.	ARO	1/18/20X3	C.3.3

No.	Audit Procedure	By	Date	WP Ref. #
C.4	**Perform cash testing—bank confirmations.**			
	A. Obtain the December bank reconciliations for significant cash/bank accounts.	ARO	2/8/20X3	C.4.1-4.2
	B. Perform the following procedures to complete substantive testing on the December bank reconciliation:			
	i. Test the reconciliation for clerical accuracy.	ARO	2/8/20X3	C.4.1-4.2
	ii. Tie the reconciliation to the Trial Balance (TB): Tie the balance per the GL on the bank reconciliation to the TB.	ARO	2/8/20X3	C.4.2, A.1.9
	iii. Tie the balance per the bank to the cash bank confirmation.	ARO	2/8/20X3	C.4.2, C.3.3
	iv. Tie the outstanding checks to the outstanding check listing.	ARO	2/8/20X3	C.4.2-4.3
	v. Test the deposits in transit: Trace the deposits in transit to the January cutoff bank statement, December cash receipts journal, December mailroom control listing, daily deposit slips, and validated bank receipts.	ARO	2/8/20X3	C.4.2-4.3, C.4.5, C.4.7
	1. Obtain the January cutoff bank statement directly from bank.	ARO	2/8/20X3	C.4.5
	vi. Test other items: Tie any bank fees, interest earned, or other reconciling items to the December bank statement.	ARO	2/8/20X3	C.4.2, C.4.4
	C. Test the outstanding checks on the December bank reconciliation as follows:			
	i. Trace the total of outstanding checks from the reconciliation to the outstanding checks listing.	ARO	2/8/20X3	C.4.2-4.3
	ii. Trace the outstanding checks (date, amount, check number) from the outstanding check listing to clearance on the January cutoff bank statement.	ARO	2/8/20X3	C.4.2-4.3, C.4.5
	iii. Reconcile the outstanding check register from December by beginning with the outstanding checks total for November, adding checks written during December from the client's check log (operating account) records, and subtracting checks clearing on the bank statement in December.	ARO	2/8/20X3	C.4.3-4.4, C.4.6, C.4.8
	iv. Investigate any checks that still are outstanding from the November outstanding check register.	ARO	2/8/20X3	C.4.3, C.4.6
	D. Note any unusual items.	ARO	2/8/20X3	C.4.1

No.	Audit Procedure	By	Date	WP Ref. #
C.5	**Inquiry of management.**			
	A. Discuss with management any related party transactions that would affect cash transactions and any restrictions on cash.	ARO	2/9/20X3	C.5.1
	B. Determine if any of the above items require disclosure.	ARO	2/9/20X3	C.5.1
AR.1	**Understanding internal controls over the sales, accounts receivable, and allowance processes.**			
	A. Interview appropriate personnel to understand the sales, accounts receivable, and allowance processes.	TES	01/17/20X3	AR.1.1
	B. Document the interview and responses in a narrative and a flowchart.	TES	01/17/20X3	AR.1.2
	C. Perform a walkthrough of the process and document your understanding of the internal controls.	TES	01/17/20X3	AR.1.1
AR.2	**Test internal controls over the accounts receivable and sales processes.**			
	A. Select a random sample of recorded sales from the sales journal to test internal controls over accounts receivable and sales processes. Use attribute sampling to calculate the sample size.	TES	01/23/20X3	AR.2.1-2.2
	B. For each item in the sample, obtain the customer purchase order, sales order, shipping documents, and copy of the sales invoice. Reperform the client's internal control procedures by comparing the quantity, price, and dates on the customer purchase orders, approved sales orders, shipping documents, and sales invoices.	TES	01/23/20X3	AR.2.2-2.4
	C. Follow up on any exceptions or deviations noted to determine if they are internal control weaknesses and whether the client has remedied them.	TES	01/23/20X3	AR.2.2-2.4
	D. Use attribute sampling procedures to evaluate the results and conclude whether the internal controls over accounts receivable and sales are operating effectively.	TES	01/23/20X3	AR.2.1

No.	Audit Procedure	By	Date	WP Ref. #
AR.3	**Perform substantive analytical procedures.**			
	A. Create an analysis comparing prior year sales, AR, and allowance balances to current year. Calculate both the $ change and % change from prior year. Analyze sales by product and perform additional ratio analysis.	TES	02/10/20X3	AR.3.1-3.4
	B. Reconcile the amounts on the lead sheet to the Trial Balance.	TES	02/10/20X3	AR.3.1-3.2
	C. Identify any fluctuations greater than the tolerable misstatement (TM) threshold and greater than a 10% change.	TES	02/10/20X3	AR.3.1-3.4
	D. Discuss significant fluctuations with the client and substantiate client explanations.	TES	02/10/20X3	AR.3.1-3.4
AR.4	**Test the detailed listing of the aged accounts receivable balances (aged by customer name).**			
	A. Trace the totals from the AR Aging Schedule to the AR Lead Sheet.	TES	02/12/20X3	AR.4.1-4.2
	B. Randomly select 2 account balances in each aging category and agree to supporting documentation to verify the balance is included in the proper aging category. → 11/17/20X2 cupcakes were returned	TES	02/12/20X3	AR.4.1-4.5
	C. Investigate any significant amounts greater than 120 days for collectability.	TES	02/12/20X3	AR.4.1-4.2
AR.5	**Send positive accounts receivable confirmation letters.**			
	A. Select the 5 largest AR account balances from the AR Aging Schedule. → The Sandwich place is not our	TES	02/01/20X3	AR.5.1
	B. Set up a confirmation worksheet to keep track of the dates confirmations are sent, resent, and received. Document findings and any issues in the worksheet.	TES	02/01/20X3	AR.5.1
	C. Have client prepare and sign confirmations.	TES	02/01/20X3	AR.5.2
	D. Maintain control of the confirmation process. The audit team should mail the confirmations and receive them directly.	TES	02/01/20X3	AR.5.1
	i. Include prepaid self-addressed envelopes with the confirmations so that we receive them at our audit offices.	TES	02/01/20X3	AR.5.1

No.	Audit Procedure	By	Date	WP Ref. #
AR.5	**Send positive accounts receivable confirmation letters (continued).**			
	E. Reconcile the returned confirmation to the AR account balances on the AR Aging Schedule.	TES	02/01/20X3	AR.5.1-5.8
	i. Investigate any differences between the confirmation and the AR Aging Schedule and document any needed adjustments.	TES	02/01/20X3	AR.5.1-5.8
	ii. For confirmations not received, perform additional testing, including reviewing subsequent payments and examining supporting documentation (shipping documents, sales invoices, and customers' purchase orders).	TES	02/01/20X3	AR.5.1-5.8
	F. Review confirmations for any indication of lack of ability to pay balances (tie to allowance procedures) or dispute over amounts that could lead to uncollectible balances.	TES	02/01/20X3	AR.5.1-5.8
AR.6	**Perform year-end sales cutoff tests.**			
	A. Select 2 customers and examine their transactions in the 5 days before year end and the 5 days after year end.	TES	02/13/20X3	AR.6.1-6.7
	B. Vouch the transactions to the proper shipping reports and sales invoices. Verify that the transactions were recorded in the proper period.	TES	02/13/20X3	AR.6.1-6.7
	C. Identify if any unusual changes to shipping terms occurred just before year end.	TES	02/13/20X3	AR.6.1-6.7
AR.7	**Evaluate the allowance for uncollectible accounts.**			
	A. Evaluate the client's policy for setting an estimate on collecting overdue accounts. Investigate any changes from prior year.	TES	02/14/20X3	AR.7.1
	B. Evaluate the collectability of significant AR balances by reviewing subsequent payments.	TES	02/14/20X3	AR.7.1
	C. Develop our own estimate and compare to the client's.	TES	02/14/20X3	AR.7.1
	i. Compare both the dollar amount and estimate of uncollectability for each aging category to prior year's balances and estimates of uncollectability percentages.	TES	02/14/20X3	AR.7.1
	ii. Select and review the 5 largest customer accounts. Review for late payments, credit ratings and approval, and any unusual transactions through the year—especially at year end.	TES	02/14/20X3	AR.7.1

No.	Audit Procedure	By	Date	WP Ref. #
AR.7	**Evaluate the allowance for uncollectible accounts (continued).**			
	D. Discuss with credit manager any large accounts that are greater than 90 days past due to understand the Company's actions for collection and the probability of receiving payment.	*TES*	*02/14/20X3*	*AR.7.1*
	E. Perform ratio analysis: Allowance balance per aging category compared to prior year; number of days' sales in AR compared to prior year; allowance balance divided by total accounts receivable compared to prior year ratio; and allowance balance divided by net credit sales compared to prior year.	*TES*	*02/14/20X3*	*AR.7.1*

Garcia and Foster, CPAs
1790 Lawrence St., Denver, CO 80202

Client: *Alpine Cupcakes, Inc.*
Year End: *12/31/20X2*

Position	Name	Initials	Sign Off	Experience	Client responsibilities
Partner	Anna Garcia	AAG	AAG	30 years	Overall review and key discussions
Partner	Evan Foster	EMF	EMF	30 years	Second partner review
Sr. Manager	Tryg Johnson	TKJ	TKJ	15 years	Overall review, meetings and discussion with key executives
Manager	Simon Malik	SDM	SDM	8 years	Review AR/Sales, review Inventory, review Payroll
Senior	Tracey Smith	TES	TES	3 years	AR/Sales, review Cash, PP&E, and AP
Staff 2	Sachdev Gupta	SNG	SNG	2 years	Inventory and AP
Staff	Kaleem Adams	KJA	KJA	Less than one year	PP&E, Payroll
Staff	Alicia Ortiz	ARO	ARO	Less than one year	Cash audit procedures

Documentation and Review Guidelines
The firm requires all workpaper documents to include proper signoff by both the preparer and reviewer for each section of the audit. The workpapers should include a tickmark legend that clearly references and explains each tickmark used in the document. Workpaper reference numbering should be included in the bottom right hand corner of the document, align with the audit program and be prepared in sequential order. All documents prepared by a lower level audit staff member should be reviewed within 10 business days of signoff by the auditor preparing the document.

Alpine Cupcakes, Inc.
Engagement Letter
Audit Year December 31, 20X2

| Performed by: |
| TES 02/25/20X3 |
| Reviewed by: |
| TKJ 2/25/20X3 |

Garcia and Foster, CPAs, LLC
1790 Lawrence St., Denver, CO 80202

November 1, 20X2

Alexis Madison, President and CEO
Alpine Cupcakes Inc.
1250 16th ST
Denver CO 80202

Dear Ms. Madison,

The purpose of this letter is to confirm our understanding of the arrangements for our audit of Alpine Cupcakes, Inc.

You have requested that we audit the financial statements of Alpine Cupcakes, Inc., which comprise the balance sheets as of December 31, 20X2 and 20X1, and the related statements of income, stockholders' equity, and cash flows for each of the three years in the period ended December 31, 20X2. We are pleased to confirm our acceptance and our understanding of this audit engagement by means of this letter. Our audit will be conducted with the objective of our expressing an opinion on the financial statements.

We will conduct our audit in accordance with the standards of the Public Company Accounting Oversight Board. These standards require that we plan and perform the audit to obtain reasonable assurance about whether the financial statements are free of material misstatement, whether caused by error or fraud. Accordingly, there is some risk that a material misstatement would remain undetected. Although not absolute assurance, reasonable assurance is a high level of assurance. A financial statement audit is not designed to detect error or fraud that is immaterial to the financial statements. An audit also includes evaluating the appropriateness of accounting policies used and the reasonableness of significant accounting estimates made by management, as well as evaluating the overall presentation of the financial statements. If, for any reason, we are unable to complete the audit or are unable to form an opinion, we may decline to express an opinion or decline to issue a report as a result of the engagement.

In conducting our audit, we consider internal control relevant to the entity's preparation and fair presentation of the financial statements in order to design audit procedures that are appropriate in the circumstances but not for the purpose of expressing an opinion on the effectiveness of the entity's internal control. The Company is not required to have, nor are we engaged to perform, an audit of its internal control over financial reporting. However, we will communicate to you in writing concerning any significant deficiencies or material weaknesses in internal control relevant to the audit of the financial statements that we have identified during the audit.

Garcia and Foster Audit Workpaper

A.1.1: pg. 1 of 2

Our audit will be conducted on the basis that you acknowledge and understand that you have responsibility:

a. for the preparation and fair presentation of the financial statements, including disclosures in accordance with accounting principles generally accepted in the United States of America;

b. for the design, implementation, and maintenance of internal control relevant to the preparation and fair presentation of financial statements that are free from material misstatement, whether due to fraud or error;

c. for identifying and ensuring that the company complies with the laws and regulations applicable to its activities; and

d. to provide us with
   i. access to all information of which you are aware that is relevant to the preparation and fair presentation of the financial statements such as records, documentation, and other matters;
   ii. additional information that we may request from you for the purpose of the audit; and
   iii. unrestricted access to persons within the entity from whom we determine it necessary to obtain audit evidence.

At the conclusion of the engagement, you will provide us with a letter that confirms certain representations made during the audit. You are responsible for adjusting the financial statements to correct material misstatements relating to accounts or disclosures, and for affirming to us in the representation letter that the effects of any uncorrected misstatements are immaterial, both individually and in the aggregate, to the financial statements taken as a whole.

We will issue a written report upon completion of our audit of Alpine Cupcakes, Inc.'s financial statements. Our report will be addressed to the shareholders and board of directors of Alpine Cupcakes, Inc. We cannot provide assurance that an unmodified opinion will be expressed. Circumstances may arise in which it is necessary for us to modify our opinion, add an emphasis-of-matter or other-matter paragraph(s), or withdraw from the engagement.

We will bill for these services monthly at our regular per diem rates, plus travel and any additional out-of-pocket expenses.

Please sign and return the attached copy of this letter to indicate your acknowledgment of, and agreement with, the arrangements for our audit of the financial statements including our respective responsibilities.

Very truly yours,
Anna Garcia, CPA
Garcia and Foster, CPAs, LLC

Acknowledged and agreed on behalf of Alpine Cupcakes, Inc.
Signed: *Alexis Madison*
Name and Title: Alexis Madison, President and CEO, Alpine Cupcakes, Inc.
Date: November 19, 20X2

Alpine Cupcakes, Inc.
Management Representation Letter
Audit Year December 31, 20X2

Performed by:
TES 02/25/20X3
Reviewed by:
TKJ 2/25/20X3

ALPINE CUPCAKES, INC.
1250 16th ST, Denver CO 80202

February 19, 20X3

Garcia and Foster, CPAs, LLC
1790 Lawrence St., Denver, CO 80202

This representation letter is provided in connection with your audit of the financial statements of Alpine Cupcakes, Inc., which includes the balance sheets as of December 31, 20X2 and 20X1, and the related statements of income, stockholders' equity, and cash flows for each of the three years in the period ended December 31, 20X2, for the purpose of expressing an opinion on whether the financial statements are presented fairly, in all material respects, in accordance with accounting principles generally accepted in the United States (U.S. GAAP).

Certain representations in this letter are described as being limited to matters that are material. Items are considered material, regardless of size, if they involve an omission or misstatement of accounting information that, in light of the surrounding circumstances, makes it probable that the judgment of a reasonable person relying on the information would be changed or influenced by the omission or misstatement.

Except where otherwise stated below, immaterial matters less than $1,000 collectively are not considered to be exceptions that require disclosure for the purpose of the following representations. This amount is not necessarily indicative of amounts that would require adjustment to or disclosure in the financial statements.

We confirm that, to the best of our knowledge and belief, having made such inquiries as we considered necessary for the purpose of appropriately informing ourselves as of February 19, 20X3:

Financial Statements
- We have fulfilled our responsibilities, as set out in the terms of the audit engagement dated with our signature on November 19, 20X2, for the preparation and fair presentation of the financial statements in accordance with U.S. GAAP.
- We acknowledge our responsibility for the design, implementation, and maintenance of internal control relevant to the preparation and fair presentation of financial statements that are free from material misstatement, whether due to fraud or error.
- We acknowledge our responsibility for the design, implementation, and maintenance of internal control to prevent and detect fraud.
- Significant assumptions used by us in making accounting estimates, including those measured at fair value, are reasonable.
- Related party relationships and transactions have been appropriately accounted for and disclosed in accordance with the requirements of U.S. GAAP.
- All events subsequent to the date of the financial statements and for which U.S. GAAP requires adjustment or disclosure have been adjusted or disclosed.

Client Supporting Document

A.1.2: pg. 1 of 2

Alpine Cupcakes, Inc.
Management Representation Letter
Audit Year December 31, 20X2

Performed by:
TES 02/25/20X3
Reviewed by:
TKJ 2/25/20X3

Financial Statements (continued)

- The effects of uncorrected misstatements are immaterial, both individually and in the aggregate, to the financial statements as a whole. A list of the uncorrected misstatements is attached to the representation letter.
- The effects of all known actual or possible litigation and claims have been accounted for and disclosed in accordance with U.S. GAAP.

Information Provided

- We have provided you with:
  - Access to all information of which we are aware that is relevant to the preparation and fair presentation of the financial statements such as records, documentation, and other matters;
  - Additional information that you have requested from us for the purpose of the audit; and
  - Unrestricted access to persons within the entity from whom you determined it necessary to obtain audit evidence.
- All transactions have been recorded in the accounting records and are reflected in the financial statements.
- We have disclosed to you the results of our assessment of the risk that the financial statements may be materially misstated as a result of fraud.
- We have no knowledge of any fraud or suspected fraud that affects the entity and involves:
  - Management;
  - Employees who have significant roles in internal control; or
  - Others when the fraud could have a material effect on the financial statements.
- We have no knowledge of any allegations of fraud, or suspected fraud, affecting the entity's financial statements communicated by employees, former employees, analysts, regulators, or others.
- We have disclosed to you all known instances of noncompliance or suspected noncompliance with laws and regulations whose effects should be considered when preparing financial statements.
- We are not aware of any pending or threatened litigation, claims, and assessments whose effects should be considered when preparing the financial statements, and we have not consulted legal counsel concerning litigation, claims, or assessments.
- We have disclosed to you the identity of Alpine Cupcakes, Inc.'s related parties and all the related party relationships and transactions of which we are aware.

Alexis Madison

Alexis Madison, President and CEO, Alpine Cupcakes, Inc.
February 19, 20X3

Report of Independent Registered Public Accounting Firm

TO: Shareholders and Board of Directors, Alpine Cupcakes, Inc.

We have audited the accompanying balance sheets of Alpine Cupcakes, Inc., as of December 31, 20X2 and 20X1, and the related statements of income, stockholders' equity, and cash flows for each of the three years in the period ended December 31, 20X2. These financial statements are the responsibility of the Company's management. Our responsibility is to express an opinion on these financial statements based on our audits.

We conducted our audits in accordance with the standards of the Public Company Accounting Oversight Board (United States). Those standards require that we plan and perform the audit to obtain reasonable assurance about whether the financial statements are free of material misstatement. The Company is not required to have, nor were we engaged to perform, an audit of its internal control over financial reporting. Our audits included consideration of internal control over financial reporting as a basis for designing audit procedures that are appropriate in the circumstances, but not for the purpose of expressing an opinion on the effectiveness of the Company's internal control over financial reporting. Accordingly, we express no such opinion. An audit also includes examining, on a test basis, evidence supporting the amounts and disclosures in the financial statements, assessing the accounting principles used and significant estimates made by management, as well as evaluating the overall financial statement presentation. We believe that our audits provide a reasonable basis for our opinion.

In our opinion, the financial statements referred to above present fairly, in all material respects, the financial position of the Company as of December 31, 20X2 and 20X1, and the results of its operations, stockholders' equity, and its cash flows for the period ended December 31, 20X2, in conformity with U.S. generally accepted accounting principles.

Garcia and Foster, CPAs, LLC

Denver, CO
February 25, 20X3

Performed by:
TES 02/25/20X3
Reviewed by:
TKJ 2/25/20X3

PBC

Balance Sheet:	December 31, 20X2	December 31, 20X1
Current Assets		
Cash: Storefront	$124,473.95 TB	$135,135.15 PY
Cash: Corporate Accounts	441,786.75	212,976.82
Cash: Payroll	123,227.85	124,726.15
Accounts Receivable	195,120.87	191,451.64
Office Supplies	1,726.00	2,604.00
Cooking Supplies	4,090.00	4,713.00
Inventory: Ingredients	22,053.14	25,580.09
Inventory: Cake Boxes and Cupcake Cups	2,165.65	1,190.10
Inventory: Beverages	4,224.00	3,260.80
Total Current Assets	**$918,868.21**	**$701,637.75**
Long-Term Assets		
Equipment	150,180.00 TB	150,180.00
Accumulated Depreciation: Equipment	(93,336.00)	(78,828.00)
Plant & Property	330,000.00	330,000.00
Accumulated Depreciation: Plant & Property	(92,400.00)	(79,200.00)
Land	125,000.00	125,000.00
Total Long-Term Assets	**$419,444.00**	**$447,152.00**
Total Assets	**$1,338,312.21**	**$1,148,789.75**
Liabilities		
Accounts Payable	37,691.60 TB	38,556.70
Wage Taxes Payable	0.00	0.00
Corporate Income Tax Payable	41,477.88	38,125.96
Dividends Payable	15,750.00	13,125.00
Mortgage Payable	285,788.21	292,262.13
Notes Payable: Vehicles	15,393.70	24,878.31
Total Liabilities	**$396,101.39**	**$406,948.10**
Stockholders' Equity		
Common Stock, Par value $1.00; Authorized 1,000,000 shares; Issued and outstanding 50,000 shares	50,000.00 TB	50,000.00
Additional Paid in Capital	120,921.00	120,921.00
Retained Earnings	771,289.82	570,920.65
Total Stockholders' Equity	**$942,210.82**	**$741,841.65**
Total Liabilities and Stockholders' Equity	**$1,338,312.21**	**$1,148,789.75**
	F	F

Tickmark Legend

TB – *Tied to December Trial Balance at A.1.9.*

PY – *Tied to prior year audit workpapers.*

F – *Footed.*

Client Financial Statement and Footnotes

A.1.4: pg. 1 of 1

Alpine Cupcakes, Inc.
Income Statements for the 12 Months Ended
12/31/20X2, 12/31/20X1, and 12/31/20X0 (USD $)

Performed by: TES 02/25/20X3
Reviewed by: TKJ 2/25/20X3

	12 Months Ended December 31, 20X2	12 Months Ended December 31, 20X1	12 Months Ended December 31, 20X0
Revenue			
Sales Revenue: Corporate Accounts	$1,465,488.42 TB	$1,400,349.58 PY	$776,593.05 PY
Sales Revenues: Storefront	349,820.50	345,317.00	287,886.09
Total Sales Revenue	**$1,815,308.92**	**$1,745,666.58**	**$1,064,479.14**
Cost of Goods Sold: Ingredients	275,649.21 TB	264,716.87	261,591.68
Cost of Goods Sold: Boxes and Cupcake Cups	16,093.95	15,389.90	5,026.65
Cost of Goods Sold: Beverages	23,390.80	23,081.20	6,929.07
Total COGS	**$315,133.96**	**$303,187.97**	**$273,547.39**
Gross Profit	**$1,500,174.96**	**$1,442,478.61**	**$790,931.75**
Interest Revenue	320.00 TB	306.00	299.63
Gross Profit Plus Interest Revenue	**$1,500,494.96**	**$1,442,784.61**	**$791,231.38**
Expenses			
Wage Expense	869,372.00 TB	866,004.00	329,465.62
Tax Expense	58,032.08	57,829.08	11,382.85
Medical Insurance Expense	32,400.00	32,400.00	25,631.85
Auto Insurance Expense	4,140.00	4,140.00	4,121.40
Interest Expense	15,673.47	16,492.92	6,684.82
Electrical & Gas Service Expense	6,563.20	6,736.80	5,552.53
Liability Insurance Expense	14,862.40	14,805.20	4,462.71
Telecommunications Expense	1,762.50	1,821.00	1,387.80
Cell Phone Service Expense	3,834.00	3,660.00	2,530.50
Postage Expense	538.65	555.75	383.79
Professional Services Expense	8,311.00	8,437.50	3,262.25
Maintenance Expense	4,712.00	4,716.00	2,335.09
Office Supplies Expense	31,553.00	30,196.00	11,720.37
Dry Cleaning Expense	1,671.85	1,703.75	1,224.46
Storefront Paper Supplies Expense	3,148.75	3,374.25	428.27
Rental Expense	19,008.00	19,008.00	11,784.81
Waste Services Expense	600.00	600.00	447.04
Car Maintenance and Fuel Expense	3,956.40	3,956.40	3,010.55
Repair Expense	1,458.75	1,508.75	967.84
Water Expense	1,536.25	1,557.50	1,339.52
Soda Machine Repair and CO2 Expense	4,680.00	4,728.00	2,852.89
Credit Card Expense	3,760.36	3,714.30	2,648.22
Cooking Supplies Expense	52,199.00	47,745.00	27,045.65
Banking Fees	1,560.00	1,560.00	66.12
Selling and Administrative Expenses	**$1,145,333.66**	**$1,137,250.20**	**$460,736.95**
Depreciation Expense: Equipment	14,508.00 TB	16,608.00	16,608.00
Depreciation Expense: Plant & Property	13,200.00	13,200.00	13,200.00
Total Depreciation Expense	**$27,708.00**	**$29,808.00**	**$29,808.00**

Client Financial Statements and Footnotes

A.1.5: pg. 1 of 2

Performed by:
TES 02/25/20X3
Reviewed by:
TKJ 2/25/20X.

PBC	12 Months Ended December 31, 20X2	12 Months Ended December 31, 20X1	12 Months Ended December 31, 20X0	
Total Expenses	$1,173,041.66	$1,167,058.20	PY $490,544.95	PY
Earnings Before Income Taxes	$327,453.30	$275,726.41	$300,686.42	
Income Tax Expense	111,334.13 TB	93,746.98	102,233. 38	
Net Income	$216,119.17	$181,979.43	$198,453.04	
F				
Earnings Per Share	$4.32 β	$3.64 PY	$3.97 PY	

Tickmark Legend

TB – *Tied to December Trial Balance at A.1.9.*

PY – *Tied to prior year audit workspapers.*

F – *Footed.*

β – *Recalculated without exception.*

Alpine Cupcakes, Inc.
Statements of Stockholders' Equity for the Years Ended
12/31/20X2 and 12/31/20X1 (USD $)

| | Common Stock | | Additional | Retained | Accumulated Other Comprehensive | Total Shareholders' |
	Shares	Par Value	Paid-in Capital	Earnings	Income/(Loss)	Equity
Balances as of January 1, 20X0	50,000	$50,000.00	$120,921.00	$203,613.18	$0.00	$374,534.18
Net Income	-	-	-	198,453.04	-	198,453.04
Dividends declared	-	-	-	-	-	-
Common Stock issued	-	-	-	-	-	-
Balances as of December 31, 20X0	50,000	50,000.00	120,921.00	402,066.22	0.00	572,987.22
Net Income	-	-	-	181,979.43	-	181,979.43
Dividends declared	-	-	-	(13,125.00)	-	(13,125.00)
Common Stock issued	-	-	-	-	-	-
Balances as of December 31, 20X1	50,000	50,000.00	120,921.00	570,920.65	0.00	741,841.65
Net Income	-	-	-	216,119.17	-	216,119.17
Dividends declared	-	-	-	(15,750.00)	-	(15,750.00)
Common Stock issued	-	-	-	-	-	-
Balances as of December 31, 20X2	50,000	$50,000.00	$120,921.00	$771,289.82	$0.00	$942,210.82

PY →

F

1
2
3

Tickmark Legend

PY – Tied to prior year audit workpapers.

F – Footed.

1 – Tied Net Income to the Income Statement for current year at A.1.5.

2 – Tied Dividends Declared to board meeting minutes.

3 – No new common stock issuance in current year per discussion with client and review of board meeting minutes.

Performed by:
TES 02/25/20X3
Reviewed by:
TKJ 2/25/20X3

PBC

	12 Months Ended December 31, 20X2	12 Months Ended December 31, 20X1	12 Months Ended December 31, 20X0
Net Income	$216,119.17 *1*	$181,979.43 PY	$198,453.04 PY
Cash Flows from Operations			
Depreciation Expense: Equipment	$14,508.00 TB	$16,608.00	$16,608.00
Depreciation Expense: Plant & Property	13,200.00	13,200.00	13,200.00
Chg Accounts Receivable	(3,669.23) β	(111,361.64)	(59,200.03)
Chg Office Supplies	878.00	(104.00)	(202.44)
Chg Cooking Supplies	623.00	(513.00)	(405.22)
Chg Inventory: Ingredients	3,526.95	(3,362.09)	(5,203.16)
Chg Inventory: Cake Boxes and Cupcake Cups	(975.55)	209.40	(1,278.03)
Chg Inventory: Beverages	(963.20)	(937.80)	(1,024.84)
Chg Accounts Payable	(865.10)	11,675.20	(1,799.08)
Chg Corporate Income Tax Payable	3,351.92	5,583.70	5,975.55
Cash Flows from Operations	$245,733.96	$112,977.20	$165,123.79
Cash Flows from Investing Activities	$0.00	$0.00	$0.00
Cash Flows from Financing Activities			
Chg Mortgage Payable	($6,473.92) β	($6,158.82)	($5,859.07)
Chg Notes Payable: Vehicles	(9,484.61)	(8,980.26)	(8,500.98)
Dividends Paid	(13,125.00)	-	-
Cash Flows from Financing Activities	($29,083.53)	($15,139.08)	($14,360.05)
Change in Cash	$216,650.43	$97,838.12	$150,763.74
Plus Beginning Cash (all cash accounts)	472,838.12 PY	375,000.00	224,236.26
Ending Cash	$689,488.55 *2*	$472,838.12	$375,000.00

F

Tickmark Legend

PY – *Tied to prior year audit workspapers.*

F – *Footed.*

β – *Recalculated without exception.*

1 – *Tied Net Income to the Income Statement for current year at A.1.5.*

2 – *Tied to total cash in balance sheet at A.1.4.*

PBC

ALPINE CUPCAKES, INC.
NOTES TO FINANCIAL STATEMENTS

1. Description of Business

Alpine Cupcakes, Inc. ("the Company") is an upscale, boutique bakery located in Denver, Colorado that focuses on the production and sale of gourmet cupcakes. Currently, about 80% of sales are to business clients and 20% are direct customer sales through a storefront in downtown Denver. Five years ago, the Company issued a limited number of shares in an IPO to raise cash for growing the business.

2. Basis of Presentation and Preparation

In the opinion of the Company's management, the accompanying financial statements reflect all adjustments, which are normal and recurring in nature, necessary for fair financial statement presentation. The preparation of these financial statements in conformity with U.S. generally accepted accounting principles ("GAAP") requires management to make estimates and assumptions that affect the amounts reported in these financial statements and accompanying notes. Actual results could differ materially from those estimates. The Company's fiscal year is the 12-month period that ends on December 31, with quarters ending on March 31, June 30, and September 30.

3. Revenue Recognition

Net sales consist primarily of revenue from the sale of cupcakes and beverages. The Company recognizes revenue when persuasive evidence of an arrangement exists, delivery has occurred, the sales price is fixed or determinable and collection is probable. The Company considers the product delivered when storefront purchases occur or customer deliveries are completed. The Company defers revenue until the customer receives the product because the Company retains a portion of the risk of loss on these sales during transit. There is no significant balance of deferred revenue at year end.

4. Fair Value of Financial Instruments

The Company's financial instruments consist of cash and accounts receivable. Because of the short-term nature of these instruments, carrying value approximates fair value.

5. Inventory and Cost of Goods Sold

The Company's inventories consist primarily of raw ingredients since the Company ships finished goods immediately to a customer to retain product freshness. Inventories are accounted for using the First-in First-out method, with inventory being recorded at the lower of cost or market. Cost of sales represents costs directly related to the manufacture and distribution of products. Primary costs include ingredients and packaging.

Performed by:
TES 02/25/20X3
Reviewed by:
TKJ 2/25/20X3

6. Accounts Receivable—Trade

In the normal course of business, the Company extends credit to corporate customers that satisfy predefined credit criteria, based upon the results of management's recurring financial account reviews and evaluation of current and projected economic conditions. As of December 31, no customer balance comprises more than 11% of year-end accounts receivable and only 3% of trade receivables are more than 30 days overdue. Thus, management believes the Company has little concentration of credit risk associated with its customer base. The Company uses the direct write-off method of accounting for uncollectible accounts, and thus does not have an allowance for uncollectible accounts. The Company has written off only one account in the prior 2 years due to careful credit screening of customers.

6. Property, Plant, and Equipment

The Company records property, plant, and equipment at cost and depreciates the assets on a straight-line basis over the estimated useful lives of the assets. Estimated useful lives are 5 to 10 years for machinery and equipment and 25 years for buildings and related improvements. The Company expenses maintenance and repairs as incurred. Management reviews long-lived assets for impairment whenever events or changes in circumstances indicate that the carrying amount of such assets may not be recoverable.

6. Debt

As of December 31, the Company had $301,182 in notes outstanding with a weighted average interest rate of 5%. Time to maturity for long-term debt is 20 years for the mortgage, and an average of 3.5 years for equipment notes. Company policy of paying account payable obligations in a timely manner results in no significant outstanding debt with vendors.

Long-term debt consists of the following:

Description		12/31/20X2	12/31/20X1	
5% note due in 18 years	A.1.4	$285,788	$292,262	P
5% and 6% notes due in 6 years and 3 years, respectively		$15, 394	$24,878	

The following table provides details on the current portion of the mortgage and notes payable. The current portion of notes payable has significantly decreased because the Company paid off a loan on the delivery van during 20X2.

		Mortgage--Bakery			Notes Payable--Vans	
		As of 12/31/20X2	As of 12/31/20X1		As of 12/31/20X2	As of 12/31/20X1
Current payable		6,805.14	6,473.92		4,811.38	9,484.61
Long-term payable		278,983.07	285,788.21		10,582.32	15,393.70
Total payable	A.1.4	285,788.21	PY 292,262.13	A.1.4	15,393.70	PY 24,878.31

Interest expense for the years ending December 31, 20X2, 20X1 and 20X0 was $15,673, $16,493 and $6,685, respectively.

A.1.5   PY

PY

Alpine Cupcakes, Inc.
Trial Balance
December 31, 20X2

Performed by:
TES 02/25/20X3
Reviewed by:
TKJ 2/25/20X3

PBC

Account No.	Description	Dr	Cr
1100	Cash: Storefront	$124,473.95 A.1.4	
1101	Cash: Corporate Accounts *C.4.2*	441,786.75	
1102	Cash: Payroll	123,227.85	
1200	Accounts Receivable	195,120.87	
1250	Office Supplies	1,726.00	
1260	Cooking Supplies	4,090.00	
1600	Inventory: Ingredients	22,053.14	
1610	Inventory: Cake Boxes and Cupcake Cups	2,165.65	
1620	Inventory: Beverages	4,224.00	
1300	Equipment	150,180.00	
1400	Accumulated Depreciation: Equipment		93,336.00 A.1.4
1310	Plant & Property	330,000.00	
1410	Accumulated Depreciation: Plant & Property		92,400.00
1320	Land	125,000.00	
2200	Accounts Payable		37,691.60
2100-2105	Wage Taxes Payable		-
2400	Mortgage Payable		285,788.21
2500	Notes Payable: Vehicles		15,393.70
2600	Corporate Income Tax Payable		41,477.88
2700	Dividends Payable		15,750.00
3100	Common Stock		50,000.00
3200	Additional Paid in Capital		120,921.00
3110	Retained Earnings (beginning less 20X2 dividends)		555,170.65
4100	Sales Revenue: Corporate Accounts		1,465,488.42
4101	Sales Revenues: Storefront		349,820.50
5000	Cost of Goods Sold: Ingredients	275,649.21 A.1.5	
5010	Cost of Goods Sold: Boxes and Cupcake Cups	16,093.95	
5020	Cost of Goods Sold: Beverages	23,390.80	
4102	Interest Revenue		320.00 A.1.5
6200	Wage Expense	869,372.00	
6201-6205	Wage Tax Expense	58,032.08	
6207	Federal Income Tax Expense	111,334.13	
7001	Medical Insurance Expense	32,400.00	
7002	Auto Insurance Expense	4,140.00	
7003	Interest Expense	15,673.47	
7004	Electrical & Gas Service Expense	6,563.20	
7005	Liability Insurance Expense	14,862.40	

Client Supporting Document

A.1.9: pg. 1 of 2

31

Alpine Cupcakes, Inc.
Trial Balance
December 31, 20X2

Account No.	Description	Dr	Cr
7006	Telecommunications Expense	1,762.50 A.1.5	
7007	Cell Phone Service Expense	3,834.00	
7010	Postage Expense	538.65	
7011	Professional Services Expense	8,311.00	
7012	Maintenance Expense	4,712.00	
7013	Office Supplies Expense	31,553.00	
7014	Dry Cleaning Expense	1,671.85	
7015	Storefront Paper Supplies Expense	3,148.75	
7016	Rental Expense	19,008.00	
7017	Waste Services Expense	600.00	
7018	Car Maintenance and Fuel Expense	3,956.40	
7019	Repair Expense	1,458.75	
7020	Water Expense	1,536.25	
7021	Soda Machine Repair and CO2 Expense	4,680.00	
7022	Credit Card Expense	3,760.36	
7023	Cooking Supplies Expense	52,199.00	
7024-7025	Banking Fees	1,560.00	
8000	Depreciation Expense: Equipment	14,508.00	
8010	Depreciation Expense: Plant & Property	13,200.00	
		$3,123,557.96	$3,123,557.96

Alpine Cupcakes, Inc. ("Alpine" or "the Company") is an upscale, boutique bakery located in Denver, Colorado. The Company was founded 10 years ago by Alexis Madison. She is a native Coloradan who loves all the outdoor activities available in the Rocky Mountains—skiing and snowboarding in the winter, hiking and rock climbing in the summer. Alexis joined her college ski club during her freshman year, and she regularly made cupcakes for her teammates. She and the other ski club members would enjoy the cupcakes together after a long day on the slopes. Friends and family began asking her to cater their weddings, anniversary parties, and other events. This side business helped put Alexis through college. After graduating from college, Alexis worked at a local CPA firm in the forensic accounting department. She continued to bake for her colleagues and friends, and would often bring cupcakes into her office on Saturdays during busy season.

About 2 years after college, Alexis entered the regional competition "Cupcake Combat" and won the grand prize—$75,000. Although she loved her work at the CPA firm, Alexis decided to use her winnings to take on her own entrepreneurial dreams. She named her business Alpine Cupcakes, Inc., and began by selling her treats in downtown Denver out of a van she called her "Cupcake Coupé." A year later, Alexis had her first big break when her friend Julie Beauregard, owner of a local lunch spot, asked Alexis to supply her restaurant with cupcakes. Other business customers soon followed. Finally, Alexis had enough business to open a retail storefront shop.

After 5 years of business, the Company experienced an increased demand for its cupcakes and Alexis decided to take the Company public to help expand the business. She created a board of directors and the board authorized that 1,000,000 shares could be issued. When the initial public offering occurred, the Company decided to issue 50,000 shares at $1.00 par value. Due to the success of the business, the Company has declared and paid dividends over the past 2 years. The Company started to issue audited financial statements at the time of the initial public offering. Because it is classified as a non-accelerated filer under regulations of the Securities and Exchange Commission, Alpine is not subject to Section 404(b) of the Sarbanes-Oxley Act of 2001. Thus, the Company is not required to obtain auditor attestation of the effectiveness of its internal controls over financial reporting.

Performed by:
TES 02/25/20X3
Reviewed by:
TKJ 2/25/20X3

Alpine Cupcakes specializes in gourmet cupcakes. Focusing on cupcakes allows Alpine to keep costs down by eliminating the need to buy specialized equipment for a larger scale bakery. The Company offers a variety of choices, including vanilla, chocolate, lemon, spice, carrot cake, red velvet, gluten-free chocolate, and almond vegan. About 80% of the Company's sales are to business clients, with the remaining 20% sold through a storefront location on the 16th Street mall in downtown Denver. Business sales are on credit while retail sales at the storefront are cash only. Alexis works closely with friends and family, including her brother-in-law, who owns Mountain Dairy. Eventually, Alexis found that the business was taking a great deal of time and she was unable to supervise the kitchen properly. At that point, Alexis hired her good friend, Gabrielle Krause, to take over the kitchen as the main chef. She taught everything she knows to Gabrielle.

Alexis continues to modify the Company's business plan and monitor the gourmet cupcake trends. Current reports indicate that the gourmet cupcake business will continue to see positive growth for the next 5 years. Alexis has a few concerns about the current condition of the business. In 20X1, sugar prices were on the rise and Alexis is hoping that prices decline in 20X2. The United States Dairy Association has predicted that dairy prices will likely increase in 20X2 since the production per cow has been decreasing in the past 3 years. Alexis continues to monitor the change in prices of other raw materials to try to prevent any pricing shocks to her business.

Next year, Alexis is planning to implement a large-scale advertising campaign to try to double Alpine's cupcake business. The Company is planning to offer a private debt issuance to cover the costs of the advertising campaign and additional baking equipment needed to increase production. Alexis discussed the Company's plans for debt issuance with the audit committee and then obtained unanimous approval from the entire board of directors.

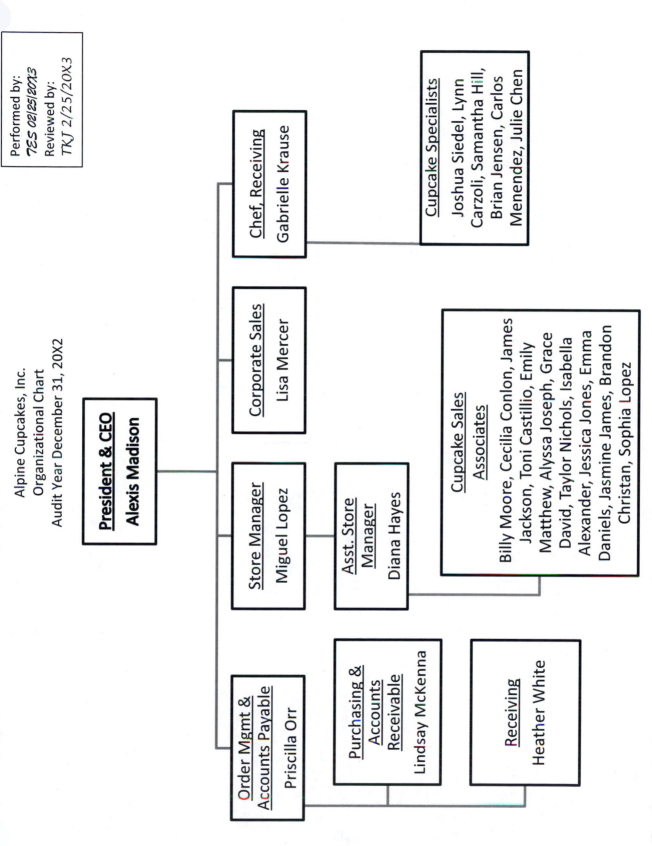

Alpine Cupcakes, Inc.
Organizational Chart
Audit Year December 31, 20X2

President & CEO
Alexis Madison

Chef, Receiving
Gabrielle Krause

Cupcake Specialists
Joshua Siedel, Lynn Carzoli, Samantha Hill, Brian Jensen, Carlos Menendez, Julie Chen

Corporate Sales
Lisa Mercer

Store Manager
Miguel Lopez

Asst. Store Manager
Diana Hayes

Cupcake Sales Associates
Billy Moore, Cecilia Conlon, James Jackson, Toni Castillio, Emily Matthew, Alyssa Joseph, Grace David, Taylor Nichols, Isabella Alexander, Jessica Jones, Emma Daniels, Jasmine James, Brandon Christan, Sophia Lopez

Order Mgmt & Accounts Payable
Priscilla Orr

Purchasing & Accounts Receivable
Lindsay McKenna

Receiving
Heather White

ORG CHART: pg. 1 of 1

Client Supporting Document

35